To a ... person

GOING FOR GOLD

British Library Cataloguing in Publication Data
Joslyn, Paul
  Going for Gold 1st Ed.
  I. Title

  ISBN 1 85609 154 6

GOING FOR GOLD

A host of simple ideas to help **you** build
your business and personal success

by

Paul Joslyn

LONDON
WITHERBY & CO. LTD
32-36 Aylesbury Street,
London EC1R 0ET

1st EDITION 1998

WITHERBY

PUBLISHERS

© Paul Joslyn
1998

ISBN 1 85609 154 6

Witherby & Co. Ltd.
32-36 Aylesbury Street
London EC1R 0ET

Tel No: 0171 251 5341
Fax No: 0171 251 1296

Forewords

Paul has always possessed a unique brand of enthusiasm that has motivated live audiences worldwide, now transferred to the printed sharing of his lifetime of sales experience.

Keith Blundell
Past President, LIA (1985/86)

I have known Paul for a number of years and have always been impressed by his enthusiasm for the cause of the financial adviser. This book conveys fully Paul's commitment and knowledge of selling skills. Any salesman - in whatever business - would gain much from studying it.

William Clark
The Rt Hon the Lord Clark of Kempston PC

Paul is an old friend I have heard speak on many occasions at LIA meetings and industry events. He never fails to inspire with his enthusiasm and warmth. His book captures in print Paul's highly inspirational talks. And not only that - if you do what he says, you will make money!

John Ellis
Public Affairs Director, Life Insurance Association

I have known Paul for many years as a friend and work colleague. He taught me many fine points in my early days as a salesman and is always quick to give credit to others. This is outlined in this book, which is a reminder of the basics of the sales process, applicable to most businesses. He credits many of the ideas to others but his personality shines through with the stories and 'Jossers' quotes. His enthusiasm is infectious.

Paul Latter
President, AXA Sunlife Top Achiever Club 1997/98

Paul is one of the most sought after speakers I know because he combines technical knowledge of the highest order, communication skills par excellence with a wonderful sense of humour and personal warmth.
Wherever Paul goes he inspires confidence and enthusiasm and this helps everyone to go forward with renewed determination and vigour.
Now, with this book, you can take a dose of Paul Joslyn medicine whenever you need it!
I commend it to you.

Jeff Travis
Chief Executive, Life Insurance Association.

Acknowledgements

I would like to thank all of those who assisted me in preparing this little book of ideas but in particular Alan Witherby and Kathleen Jenkins the publishers for their guidance, encouragement and patience.

I would also like to particularly thank Jeremy Allaway for his kind assistance in helping me prepare the book and with the scripting.

I am also grateful to Ron Secker of AXA Sun Life for allowing me to revise some of the ideas from an earlier booklet I prepared for the sales force, and for also allowing me to use some of the old ideas from earlier internal booklets.

I am grateful for the illustrations prepared by one of my dear daughters Nichola Joslyn along with David Hart, an old work colleague of mine

I am grateful to John Ellis of the Life Insurance Association for supplying some of the statistics and also allowing me to use some of the Industry Realities Campaign stories.

Contents

About the Author

Paul started in the Financial Services Industry in 1963, straight from school in High Wycombe. He was proud to join the beautiful offices of Equity and Law Life Assurance Company. After five happy years he decided he enjoyed meeting people so he became a salesman for Sun Life Assurance, another fine old insurance company based in London. He quickly became one of their most successful salesmen and helped arrange cover for many people, including the rich and famous. He subsequently specialised in pensions, sales training and sales management.

Paul holds the Chartered Insurance Institute and Life Insurance Association main Financial Services examinations. He was awarded the LIA Gold Medal for his exam success and also the Outstanding Service Award. He has been a key member of the LIA for many years and was made the President of the 26,000 strong association in April 1997 for the year ending May 1998. He is also a life member and companion of the Institute of Sales and Marketing Management.

Paul has been a popular industry speaker since 1978, speaking on all aspects of the business throughout the UK, in the USA and Europe. He is well known for his enthusiasm. As a sales trainer Paul has helped many new salesmen to build confidence and pride in our profession.

Introduction

Selling financial products is a complex web of human interaction, involving many different emotions. This booklet sets out the basics. Most simple aspects of the sales process are covered and for ease of presentation, that process has been broken down into the eight following areas:

1. **Belief**
2. **Personal Development**
3 **Prospecting Finding New Potential Clients**
4. **Approaching a Potential Client**
5. **Fact-Finding and Presenting Correct Solutions to Needs**
6. **Closing**
7. **Servicing**
8. **Little Stories and Tips**

At the end of each section you will find some real life cases from the Life Insurance Association (LIA) Industry Realities files, based on true stories given to us by practitioners. The section is called "What we are here for." These stories will tell you just that. The names and locations have been changed for reasons of confidentiality.

I do not claim that there is anything magical about any of these simple ideas nor is any of them a startling new concept. Indeed their attraction is that they have been tried and tested over the years. What they **do** have in common is good sense and the ability to help you make sales.

Some of the ideas outlined in this booklet were developed from other sales people's tips and experiences. Naturally I have also included some of my own, based on over 30 years in the sales business and from my many contacts in the Life Insurance Association.

I would emphasise that running a business has to be based on sound professional standards and the word 'selling' should be treated with respect not as a means of manipulation. Everybody has to sell at some time whether in business or personal life. Selling is about communication and delivering our goals to the satisfaction of each party. It is a great shame that the word doesn't have the same positive meaning here in the UK as it does in the USA. Be an advisor and friend, not a manipulator!

Remember that success is not the ultimate reward, happiness is often the emotional satisfaction in what we do well and the knowledge that somebody has benefitted from our expertise. I have been very fortunate in this wonderful profession of ours to have met many lovely people, both professionally and as friends. This is very much a people business and if we like people it can be very satisfying. Remember you cannot spell the word success without 'U' in it!

To succeed we need to have a balance between sound

technical and product knowledge, professional communication plus business skills, together with a positive attitude all coupled with planned activity. This booklet mainly concentrates on the communication, business and attitude aspects, leaving the other important areas to your own continual professional development, study, training and competence requirements decided by the Regulator and your own high standards.

1

BELIEF

Self-belief: it works!
"No one can cheat you out of ultimate success, but yourself"
Ralph Waldo Emerson (1803-1882)

In our great industry we need to believe in our own abilities, in our products and services, and in our clients. Belief is crucial in any field of personal achievement - go out and get it! The 1990's have seen many British success stories from different walks of life, where self-belief has played a crucial role. Take boxer Frank Bruno's Heavyweight World Championship. It was Frank's belief in himself, his determination and hard work, coupled with his personal talent, that helped to get him there. Or the British rock groups who begin by playing in pubs and find worldwide success in such a short time. It does help to have a good manager!

Life is full of potential and achievement. We all know people who have great potential but never get around to achieving anything. I remember hearing the brilliant former rugby international Will Carling speaking at an LIA Convention on Winning. He said words to the effect that five inward strengths can close the gap between potential and achievement: vision, self-belief, results orientation, courage and integrity.

We can learn a great deal from our great achievers in the areas of sport, business, entertainment and many other walks of life.

For the purpose of this book, we will describe some of these attributes as belief. With self-belief you will normally find enthusiasm and passion for the chosen field, which, coupled with hard work, talent and a certain amount of luck brings success.

"Nothing great was ever achieved without enthusiasm"
Ralph Waldo Emerson

Emerson got it right! Enthusiasm is built on passion and belief. Without enthusiasm where do we manage to obtain that inner strength necessary to produce extraordinary performance? Enthusiasm comes from the Greek words 'Eno Theo' which mean 'Inner God'. This is the life force of creative activity and achievement which breeds confidence and often happiness in us. Enthusiasm is magic and people have managed to do the most amazing feats once the passion has been fuelled. Enthusiasm coupled with the desire to do something well, in turn motivates us to achieve that goal. It is often said that NOBODY can motivate us and that is has to come from WITHIN, in some ways this is true, but in others incorrect, e.g. if we are facing a bully or adversity, we will perform well due to fear. However, the pleasure comes from our personal desire to want to do something. Although fear is a motivator it is short-term as our survival instinct will naturally try to avoid future pain.

PASSION

I remember speaking to a teenage son of a friend one day. He was talking about getting up early to go fishing, with real passion. He was so excited about the thought of his early morning adventure to the local lake. Yet that same teenager had great difficulty in getting up in the morning during the week to go to work. It reminded me that IF ONLY WE COULD PUT THE SAME PASSION INTO OUR JOBS AS WE DO INTO OUR HOBBIES, WE COULD END UP HIGHLY SUCCESSFUL. Passion fuels the energy levels to do the things we enjoy and equally, lack of passion fuels lethargy and boredom. Passion is all about INTEREST and once we are enthused we can do, learn and remember the most amazing things.

Desire: use it!
"You cannot expect life to be a thrilling adventure if it is not thrilling inside - get enthusiastic NOW!"
"You can't be a WINNER if you are a WHINER"

Napoleon Hill, one of the masters of positive thinking, said that:
"The starting point of all achievement is desire".
Before you can convince anyone else of the value of the services you offer and of your value as a financial services adviser you must believe in yourself. Be yourself. You are unique! Use your strengths to good effect. Most people enjoy pleasurable motivation and that includes a personal desire to achieve something

which they want to happen by the preparation of concise clear goals. The first step is to write down your GOALS, be realistic and carry them out. I remember a little quote which said:

"If you want to do something you will find a way. If you don't want to do it you will find an excuse". The difference between a New Year's resolution and a goal is real desire, so be action orientated and have the persistence to carry out the plan.

These desired goals can be personal or related to business. The choice is tremendous and there are many books, seminars, tapes and videos on the art of goal setting to help us focus correctly and obtain results. However, at the end of the day only your desire to do something will give you the necessary energy and enthusiasm to do it. "If it is to be IT IS UP TO ME" was another useful little saying I heard at one of the many seminars I have attended, from a personal coach friend of mine.

Common sense: use it!
"When you face an OBSTACLE, look for the OPPORTUNITY, Not just the problem"

Ralph Waldo Emerson also said that "most problems can be cured by common sense." The trouble is that in my experience, common sense is not that common! There are many long-winded solutions offered by theorists on ideas to overcome what are basically very simple problems. In cases like this the strategy to solve a problem can cause confusion and salespeople can become fearful of getting to grips with the task at hand. Too much theory and not enough practice can be a big problem. Just listen to some of the academic debates or arguments about theories and how many people love to speak without any positive action. Also sadly how some people generalise or continually find fault with anything ever spoken about.

The message is: use common sense and keep it simple. Check procedures, be compliant and DO IT! Do not forget to plan your action first to avoid costly mistakes

We sometimes act before we think. I don't think you would jump from an aeroplane without first checking that the parachute and the emergency parachute were both in working order.

Planning: get started!
"Be self-reliant and all doors are open to you" Ralph Waldo Emerson

Self-reliance means self-discipline and awareness. If there are short cuts in the financial services industry they do not last long: there is simply no substitute for hard work. This is where planning comes in. Be organised. Keep all the appointments you make and get there on time. Be enthusiastic and positive. Avoid unjustified excuses and work to a plan. Live your job. Many successful people in our business are continually looking for new ideas to improve their sales performances. They enjoy their continual professional development and the opportunity to meet and help many people. Work to a balanced lifestyle, enjoy your social time, your family and your work.

Use your time to its' best advantage. Make effective use of your diary or personal organiser, there are many wonderful techno aids to help us. Plan your

work and work your plan. **Make planning a habit.**
Before you go to bed write down the two most
important tasks you have to do the next day in order
of importance. The following day start by working
on the number one priority task and do not go on to
number two until you have completed it. If you
haven't completed both tasks by the end of the day
don't worry. Carry the outstanding task forward to
the next day and you will have accomplished more
than you would have without a work plan to achieve
personal satisfaction with the work completed and a
record to prove you did it by yourself. Set aside time
each day to cover your administration, record
keeping and planning. If you are busy consider
employing somebody to help you with this key area.
There are many excellent retired people and others
who, due to personal circumstances, are forced to
work at home and would love a part-time job to help
out.

Success through Organisation

Successful selling involves the combination of many
varied skills and activities. As we know, technical
knowledge is vital as is the ability to conduct an
effective interview. A skill which is less valued,
however, is that of good organisation.

To organise is defined in my dictionary as "to prepare
for an activity, - to arrange, thereby to obtain
maximum benefit." How many people do we know
who would benefit from an increase in their
organisation? Quite a few I suspect - perhaps even
ourselves. Here are a few tips which would help you.

Organising ourselves: ten easy steps which work!

1. Tidy up, file papers and things where you (and others) can find them.
2. Set reasonable objectives, goals or targets.
3. Arrive early, leave plenty of time, relax.
4. Plan your call, journey, objective.
5. Ask others for help:-
   (a) ask for explanations from more experienced people,
   (b) attend training courses,
   (c) look for successful ideas.
6. Try to avoid criticising people (harmfully); few people like criticism and many will return the criticism in some form.
7. Smile - be pleasant and friendly, have a sense of humour, be good mannered.
8. Think of others' feelings before you do something.
9. Praise sincerely - most people like sincere appreciation.
10. Make notes to avoid straining your memory and to help future communication.

Good grooming is essential

Looking good means winning. Classic examples can be found in the political arena. For example, remember the smart, clean-shaven John F. Kennedy who won the 1963 US Presidential election. Our own Lady Margaret Thatcher and the beautiful Diana, Princess of Wales certainly knew the value of grooming. The media photographs show the smartness, of many famous people. If you arrived for an appointment with unkempt hair, wearing a smelly jacket what would the average potential investor think of your advice?

The message is: to attain credibility, look smarter than your competitor, be confident and know what you are talking about

Never underestimate the importance of how you look or behave. Your prospects make valued judgements based on their first visual impressions. Psychologists have proven that personal appearance carries more weight than you could possibly imagine in face-to-face encounters. In a people industry like ours it is absolutely crucial. **Think about your appearance. Are you dressed correctly?** Are your clothes colour co-ordinated and suitable for the occasion? Are you well groomed? How are your fingernails? Does your expression reflect warmth and sincerity? Smile, it's infectious! Although a controversial subject, it is best to avoid drinking alcohol before an interview as it may impair your reactions. Some prospects may think it wrong to smell drink on your breath. If you must smoke or drink, leave it for a social or more appropriate occasion. Another key area is personal fitness and energy levels to complete your work. There are many opportunities nowadays for exercise even for those with a busy schedule, and there are some wonderful gyms and health clubs who will help with our personal fitness. Why not join a dance club or Ramblers Association if you are able, you never know who you will meet and you may actually enjoy it!

2

PERSONAL DEVELOPMENT

Apart from the obvious need for adequate technical and product knowledge, many of us should look at our own personal skills and attitudes on a continuing basis. There is a need to examine aspects of our lives and develop the 'Complete Person' or 'Holistic Approach' to our efforts and energy. It can be dangerous to be preoccupied with one part of our lives at the expense of neglecting other essential areas such as family and friends, hobbies and spiritual peace. We can easily become WORKAHOLICS addicted to our careers at the expense of happiness.

I noticed a lovely quotation by an American called Jackson Brown: "Success is getting what you want but happiness is liking what you get." How true this is and I believe that in our business we must develop additional 'people skills' to really succeed. Skills such as EMPATHY which is basically understanding the other persons point of view. We should aim to be a caring person with sound values and belief. I am blessed with a lovely mother and father who taught me the value of goodness, honesty and kindness. Now I am older I really do thank them for their guidance. Even today, at their advanced ages, they take time to care for others by calling to see friends in distress and being available to help. They have many friends and are self-reliant.

The balance for success is based on ATTITUDE, ACTIVITY, SKILLS AND KNOWLEDGE and a good balance to one's personal life, together with the understanding of how to cope with the emotional and logical pressures from which we all suffer from time to time.

Pride in what we do

To be positive and have self-confidence we must take pride in what we do, both in our work and in our dealings with other people. People often do business with us as they trust and believe in what we do for them. Therefore we should take pride in the fact that these people have chosen to be our clients and look after them accordingly.

I have dealt with a number of death claims and felt pride, as well as sadness, when I presented the death claim cheque. Some of these claims resulted after the client had paid just a few premiums and I found the life office claims department to be most helpful and understanding.

I was also speaking to an adviser recently who told me that her brother-in-law was diagnosed with a serious illness, after only paying a few months' premiums into a critical illness plan she had set up for him in all good faith. The life office paid out over £160,000 to help him cope with the trauma of the serious illness with dignity. He certainly believed in the power of insurance and was thankful for the adviser's efforts on his behalf.

Professional preparation: study and training, the way forward

Go for it! Study and re-study the necessary examinations, read industry books, attend courses and seminars. **Learn to enjoy the necessary training and studying.** Become a professional. People buy financial advice on trust and respect. Professional qualifications on your business card speak volumes. Study is an ongoing basic skill and learning new facts every day can only add to your professionalism. Study can be enjoyable and rewarding and it can help you, through the knowledge you have gained, to help the customer.

What we are here for:

Ben was the breadwinner of a young family. He was in the process of arranging a mortgage when, tragically, he was killed. But not only that, he died before completion of the mortgage. However, the death benefit under the proposed policy was paid.

A letter from Ben's parents to the company praised their compassion and generosity, and even thanked the individual who made the arrangements, thinking of them with "the utmost appreciation and regard".

The family were able to complete their mortgage and live in a home without any mortgage debt, thanks to the insight and action taken by the financial adviser and his client.

Statistics show that many householders do not have

any form of life assurance to protect their mortgage or indeed plan for early retirement in the event of redudancy or ill health.

(Source: LIA booklet 'Living Life to the Full')

3

PROSPECTING: FINDING NEW POTENTIAL CLIENTS

Look for opportunities to make new friends all the time. Be interested in others sincerely and compassionately.

The people who need our services are all around us. How do we find them? As long as you have a good supply of prospects you will have most of the ingredients for success. Quite simply, prospects are needed to enhance our client bank when others die, move on, or we expand. Who is a prospect? The answer is almost everybody you meet and many, many more you will never meet unless you do something about it! Let us look at some sources of prospects. Always remember the code of conduct, the Data Protection Act Provisions and the importance of discretion, good manners and the effectiveness of the 'soft sell'. Many people do not like being harrassed or bothered by smooth talking sales people, but by being friendly and sincere you will usually be welcomed as there are a great many people in need of our services and products.

Personal Contacts

On a personal basis, the most obvious group of prospects are:

- your relatives, friends and former business clients
- neighbours
- friends of the family
- former employers or colleagues
- contacts through church, associations or clubs
- professional contacts
- old school or college friends.

We have a mutual interest in each others success, without wishing to take advantage of our personal relationships.

Existing Customers

We have many satisfied clients from all walks of life. You are part of this continuing success story. Existing customers need regular service, reassurance and contact. Prepare a database of the allocated client bank and deliver ongoing service to it. Satisfied customers are also a valuable source of referrals and a testament to our service levels.

Local Newspapers: as a source of information

- success stories are worthy of praise and a letter
- birth announcements: anyone proud enough to put an announcement in the local paper cares enough to think about the child's financial future
- engagements and marriages
- retirement and new appointment announcements
- job promotions: usually result in more disposable

income and broader horizons
- businesses for sale or expanding
- probate announcements
- firms awarded large contracts
- applications for licences: show expansion or opportunity
- planning applications: the house owner may be facing some financial pressure and need help

Lead Generation Lists

It is possible to purchase data lists with the names and addresses of potential leads in various areas of interest or geographically. These can be business people or householders, depending upon your request.

Registry of Births, Deaths and Marriages: as a source of information

These lists contain names, addresses and occupations of recently married couples, new births and deaths. Extreme care should be exercised when dealing with the recently bereaved.

Electoral Register

Available at any public library on demand, use it to identify: Householders in streets of medium to large private houses who are likely to be wealthy and in need of our services. Householders living on new estates who are likely to have young children, and those who will reach the age of 18 years next birthday and may be in need of financial help with their education.

Local Authority Planning Office

The names and addresses of all applicants for planning permission are available for inspection.

Directories of Companies: Dun & Bradstreet, Stubbs Gazette, Companies Registry etc.

Available from most public libraries and contain names of directors of small companies.

Yellow Pages and Trade Directories

Remember that most salesmen will start at 'A' and work through the alphabet. Others will start at 'Z' and work back. Be different, start at 'I' and contact potential clients who may have rarely been canvassed before. Trade directories can be found in public libraries and contain loads of useful information and background material. They are a gold mine of potential contacts listed in alphabetical order under trade headings. One of the most obvious places to look is the Business Market to find potential daytime calls. Just by looking through these directories one can see the potential for local business.

Trade Unions and Professional Membership Lists

Subject to the Data Protection Act Provisions, local offices of such organisations should be able to supply year books or lists which contain names, addresses and even telephone numbers of members.

Business Parks

Most business parks have a directory of the

businesses operating from the site. A telephone call may well establish the name of the managing director, the financial director or the personnel manager, or why not simply call in and ask, thereby introducing yourself at the same time.

Hospitals

Names of doctors, registrars, consultants and nurses are on display almost everywhere, but avoid bothering them whilst on duty. They are very busy people and often under considerable stress.

Law Society and Professional Body Listings

Available from your local library, these will list the names and addresses of solicitors, accountants and other professionals together with the date they passed their final examinations and any other useful fact-finding information.

Health, Fitness and Leisure Centres

The lobby of your local gym or leisure centre will usually display the squash and badminton league table ladders, complete with names and telephone numbers. Places like this are also useful to join. The benefits are twofold: as well as keeping fit, you can find excellent prospects on a low key sales basis. Many introductions to wealthy individuals have occurred at health clubs. Remember to ask if you may place your business card on the notice board, give it to interested people with pride.

Club Listings

Local golf, tennis, sailing or rugby clubs will often have lists of members on display at their centres. They also welcome sponsorship or adverts for their activities.

New Housing Estates

Builders and estate agents may be encouraged to pass on details of new home owners so that you can help them with financial planning. If not, call and see the new owners to introduce yourself, alternatively leave some advertising material about your services. Recently I responded to a leaflet placed through my door by a keen local estate agent.

Traders' Business Cards

Visit shops, businesses, factories etc. and collect business cards. Remember they are also in the sales business and appreciate help or networking.

Business Clubs

There are many clubs where professionals network and meet for lunch or breakfast. They often appreciate our talks or presentations on key subjects. Join a speakers club to practice your talks.

Young Farmers' Clubs

These are usually active in rural areas. Contact the Secretary of your nearest Young Farmers organisation, they also have a great number of social events for you to enjoy.

For Sale Signs on Houses and Businesses

These people may be in need of financial advice. They are certainly contemplating a change, as moving house can be both mentally and financially very stressful.

Driving Around

Many vans and lorries carry advertising material. Copy the names displayed when you are stuck in a traffic jam, not whilst moving! Use a dictating machine if it is difficult to use a pen or keyboard. Or if you are carrying a passenger ask them to jot down the names.

Names Above Shops and Businesses

Many streets have thriving businesses with the family name proudly displayed. Make a note of them and resolve to contact a certain number every month.

Advertising

Advertising can bring in extra prospects. Place well written company approved cards offering your compliant services in local newsagents, DIY superstores,supermarkets,community centres,hospital notice boards. Have a flyer sheet approved and printed for insertion and distribution in your local weekly free newspaper. Have drop cards approved and printed with information on mortgages, pensions etc. Distribute them around local housing estates. Advertise in your local club magazine. Other professionals do! Finally, make sure you clear all advertising material with your office or Regulatory requirements first. Check any article or advert for accuracy.

Information Superhighway - Surf the Internet

New technology can mean new prospects. Many computer literate salespeople can make contact with other like-minded individuals on the information superhighway. If you are a home computer user, your Net contacts can be potential prospects. Your fellow Net Surfers are also likely to be high net worth individuals. Arrange to meet them in person. The internet is a new way of making friends.

Target Marketing

Select a group of people with a common interest or occupation within easy reach of you at some time during the year. Make sure you, or somebody close, has experience in the particular target market so you can fully understand the general type of person and their needs.

This group could be:

- members of a particular local industry or one in which you have personal experience
- people living in a particular locality, e.g. a large village or upmarket housing estate
- members of a club e.g. a classic car club, society or association
- people who enjoy a particular sport or pastime, e.g. sailing, golf or horseriding. Frequent the places they frequent - become a regular. There is no need to oversell but be proud of the financial services industry. People usually ask what you

do for a living, tell them with pride!

- get to know their organisations and leaders e.g. union shop stewards, club officials etc.
- get to know their practices e.g. working hours, meeting places, rules etc.
- if you can get address lists, send out approved mailshots quarterly.
- invite prospects to exclusive seminars and let them know the seminar is restricted to their group so they will feel at ease with the other guests.

Qualifying Leads

It is often useful to target the market in a particular profession or job e.g. accountants, lawyers or other business people. When meeting a client, it may be worth noting and taking along names of as many people in the same business in the locality and saying something along these lines: "I intend calling on these people in the near future and as you are in the same line of business I wonder if you happen to know something about them." This is a way of semi-qualifying names you know very little about. At the end of the conversation you can ask further: "When I call these people, would you mind if I mentioned that you are a client of mine?"

How to get Referred Warm Leads

The best prospects usually come as referred 'warm' leads and most of the consistently successful members of our industry obtain their prospects from this source. Think about it, you want to meet people like your existing clients, your clients know lots of people like themselves. Prospects are more likely to give you an interview if you are recommended by one of their friends. You want to save yourself time and energy. Clients give referrals once they trust and respect your service.

The benefit of asking for referred leads is well proven, but so many sales people just don't ask because they fear rejection and they feel it might prejudice the case they have just signed up. There is nothing to fear if you follow two simple rules.

1. Do not necessarily wait until you have sold a case before asking for leads. Be proud of selling via recommendations. Tell people: "I prefer to do the majority of my business via referrals from satisfied customers."

2. Ask questions. Look for potential customers. "How long have you lived here?" "Where did you live before?" "Who lives there now?" Find out if they have any hobbies or sports and if they may know of other interested people. Ask for other potential prospects but don't be pushy. The main objective is to help your client, not be seen to be using them. Some clients are very pleased to give referrals, others are less willing. Be realistic and most satisfied customers will gladly recommend you.

Our business is built on trust and so the best referrals are to immediate family or neighbours where the client can say to them that they "know a person that can help them." Remember the AA advertisement: "but I know a man who can!"

Keep a book of satisfied customers letters.

You could also develop a simple recommendation card which states: "I have been very satisfied with the professional service offered to me by (your name) and recommend him to..." or simply note the prospect's name on one of his (or your) business cards and have your client sign it. Do not be pushy over referrals, alternatively do not be afraid to ask.

"With the range of financial services I can offer, most people could benefit from a brief meeting, whatever their circumstances." "What was the name of that person you work with?" Result: Highly qualified referred leads.

Related Business Opportunities

If you have written a policy under trust, why not ask to meet the trustees so that you can explain the policy. If you have written a company pension scheme, why not ask to see the accountant to update him or her on the scheme. Give the executor of a will a copy of the fact-find or policy information if the client agrees. AlTervatively ask your satisfied clients to recommend you. You know it makes sense .Do not make promises you may not be able to keep!

What we are here for:

A client and her husband moved to work in Bahrain. After advice from their financial adviser, the husband arranged £250,000 life insurance and £100,000 of critical illness cover to give financial security to the family in the event of the husband's death, and £24,000 per annum of permanent health insurance.

Just nine months later, and after only paying a small

amount in premiums to the life office, the couple returned to England for a holiday. Tragically the husband was killed in a car crash leaving his wife widowed with an 18 month old daughter and expecting another baby. The husband's father was moved to say to the financial adviser "Thank God for the life insurance you arranged."

I believe the person who made the referral would also have been very appreciative.

(Source: LIA booklet 'Living Life to the Full')

Tragic deaths by road accident happen every day, the statistics make frightening reading. We now see high performance cars, high stress levels and some business people working very long hours. It makes sense to insure against the possibility of unexpected death, especially when one has a young family or beneficiaries.

My Experience of Meeting New People

Any business needs a good client bank on which to build a good practice but some people make such a fuss about attracting potential customers that in the end they become frustrated and negative about the whole process. I travel extensively around the UK, Europe and the USA on both business and pleasure. One day I was travelling "cheapo class" with an airline to Boston when the chap next door to me struck up a conversation. He asked me where I was going and for what reason. We made conversation along the journey and enjoyed each others company. He turned out to be a millionaire, self-employed management consultant, chartered accountant, full of ideas and wealthy enough to be able to afford a house in Jersey as well as one in England. The moral of the story is that potential customers are everywhere we go and if we show an interest in them, very often they will do the same to us.

Belief

4

APPROACHING A POTENTIAL CLIENT

You have the name and preferably some qualifying background information. So what's next? How do you approach the prospect for an interview. Whether you choose a personal or telephone call there are a few golden rules to follow:
Stick to the point, and be professional and do it now! Avoid procrastination and excuses.

Cold Calling - Door Knocking Sales

In general this method of approaching potential clients has not been widely used for many years and can be conceived as being intrusive. Although this may be true at private homes, I believe that business people do not generally mind other business people calling direct to their offices in order to see if there is likely to be any interest in the service or product and to make a convenient appointment.   After all, business people also have to sell their wares and many understand the various prospecting methods or have studied salesmanship. I personally found the direct call to companies effective and rarely was anyone rude to me.

With all the current fears of confidence tricksters and home muggings, especially amongst elderly people, I personally feel it is unprofessional to try to sell financial services over the doorstep. Some advisers do introduce themselves to local residents in a friendly unobtrusive manner at the garden gate or local community areas to advertise their services to good effect. Our code of conduct and Regulatory requirements govern the manner of our approach and should be a sensible starting point.

Introductions

It is often better to be introduced by a friend or professional contact of the potential client than to call direct. This will help build the essential trust side of our business. If an introduction is not possible try to refer to the recommendation in your approach. If no recommendation is available mention the reason you are calling, or words to that effect.

"I have many clients in this area and wanted to introduce myself to see if there are any ways I can be of assistance to you or your family?" Have a business card and list of your services available.

"I specialise in providing life assurance protection for people who need and require it. I noticed that you have young children at the school. Perhaps you would be interested in a free financial consultation."

"We are a local firm of pensions specialists and help many people with their pension schemes. I will be delighted to help you review your arrangements if you wish."

"I find that many retired people enjoy attending local seminars and learning new aspects of finance. We are running such an event next week and you would be very welcome."

Get to the Point

With a new prospect you may only have time for a few words before you have lost their interest. Research has shown that the first few moments are important. What is your introductory line, is it to the point? Do not forget the purpose of the call - to get an appointment, to give simple information, or to confirm some point.

Don't try to sell over the telephone or on the doorstep, it can annoy the client. Introduce yourself, identifying your company, give the purpose of your call and tell the prospect where you got their name from. Keep it simple. Avoid arguing or being pushy. If the prospect says they don't want to see you, accept that it just may not be convenient for them to talk, or that they are not really interested.

Be courteous, apologise for troubling them. People generally do not like aggressive selling. Remember to treat people with respect, be professional, polite and brief.

When you plan a telephone session, try to fix the number of calls you will make and don't give up until you've make your quota. Then make two extra calls... the result will be forty extra calls each month and more appointments. Some financial advisers employ an assistant to make appointments. Some prefer to make their own. Work to your preference but make sure you are proactive and not merely reactive when times are slack.

Timing

Give the prospect options on a time and date. Suggest that the person may like to call into your office, if it is more convenient. Make it clear you don't want a great deal of the prospect's time; unless a full fact- find is required, or a detailed presentation on a complex issue.

"As you suggest I'd like to see you about your personal financial planning. I don't know if anything will come of it. When would it be convenient for you? Thursday at 9.50am is okay for me or Friday at 2.00pm. "

Prepare the prospect for the time needed. Make your voice interesting!   Do not smoke, drink or chew gum whether on the telephone or calling in person. Keep a record of your calls. Ring the prospect before the appointment to make sure everything is okay and to avoid a wasted journey. Mobile 'phones are an excellent way to inform clients of delays etc. Use common sense. Be considerate and avoid wasting the prospect's, and your time !

Handling Objections

You will meet objections. It is important, therefore, to understand why they occur! Here are some popular ones. Most are excuses as the prospect is not at that stage really interested or just too busy or preoccupied with something else. It may be he or she is being defensive as they don't really know you. It's a natural way of avoiding a conversation, we all do it from time to time.

"I'm not interested."
"I have all the insurance I need."
"My children are grown up."
"I can't afford any more insurance."
"I can do better in a Building Society."
"I've never heard of your company."
"I don't believe in life insurance."
"I don't have the time to spare."
"My brother,sister, other relative, sells insurance."
"All you insurance people are the same - I'm not in
  the market"
"I have a pension already"

Think about your response to these frequently voiced objections and plan responses which you are comfortable with. Remember most are not true but if they are genuine excuses, the prospect may simply want reassurance.

Just as prospecting must become a habit for success, so must Approaching. Allocate a part of each day to telephone approaching and avoid the fear of rejection if possible, it is usually defensive and not personal. The next call may be an appointment which results in your biggest case ever. Develop your own call-to-appointment-to sale ratios. Rejection is a lot less cutting when you know that your own statistics show you are one call nearer to an appointment. In that way, rejection is a positive factor. Have a good reason to approach people.

Tackling Fear

It is often said that the only thing to fear is fear itself. But fear is often the key reason for failure in selling. There are a number of books on the subject, but experience is the best antidote. Face the fear in easy stages. If your prospect is rude to you then ease off and understand that your approach to them may have been too aggressive. It is also possible that the prospect may have been under stress through no fault of yours.

Keys to Daytime Sales

If you are unhappy when a prospect suggests a late evening appointment, ask if it would be more convenient to meet in the daytime or at the weekend. Solicitors rarely make evening calls and a client takes time to see them, often travelling a long way for the appointment.

Good prospects for certain daytime activity are business people, hospital staff, teachers, shopkeepers, policemen, fire fighters, shift workers and bar or leisure staff. Use coffee breaks to meet prospects, deliver policies, get referred leads and make appointments for later interviews. Sometimes it is more productive to meet prospects in your office or at a local hotel or club. There are some wonderful facilities available for the price of a cup of coffee.

Breakfast or Tea Meetings Can Pay Off

Some conversational rapport is often better conducted outside the office or home. Why not suggest breakfast meetings. It's less expensive than lunch and the novelty of the idea may persuade the prospect to accept. You will not be interrupted by a telephone and you will have the rest of the day to devote to daytime activity. Some successful sales people in our industry hold breakfast meetings each week, at 7.30am, 8.30am and 9.30am on designated days and provided you have the willpower to stick to coffee and toast you too could be slim as well as highly successful! There is no need to use a very expensive hotel - you will be surprised at the number of suitable venues once you start looking.

Be 'user friendly'

Make yourself user friendly. Learn to listen. Be more interested than interesting. Do not interrupt when your prospect is talking and look for positive buying interest. Avoid arguing with your prospect, you want to win a friend not an argument. Do not use industry jargon! Nothing is more off-putting to people than feeling that they don't understand. You will sell if you are 'user friendly' and use language people understand. Try to help the prospect uncover needs and recognise the financial position.

Remember OPEN QUESTIONS result in open conversations and emotive responses CLOSED QUESTIONS result in quick responses and factual replies

Some Alternatives to the "Direct" Approach

There are other means of approach which you might find less stressful, where the prospect will contact you first.
• advertisements in magazines, newspapers or newsletters.

- mail shots - although the response rate is traditionally low
- seminar selling - the audience will be interested (that's why they accepted the invitation)
- exhibitions or local business fairs
- introductions from satisfied client, friends and professionals
- networking - building friendships through clubs or fellowships of common interest
- endorsement from Trade Unions, Associations or Companies.
- your name advertised on vehicles or sponsorship.
- your articles in trade magazines or local papers.

The important aspect of running your business is to investigate all sources of approach and be PROACTIVE.
Focused activity is the key to success, along with a positive, professional attitude

What we are here for:

Two policies taken out on the life of a young business client provided for a small sum assured of £26,000. Eight months later he committed suicide. Investigations revealed that one month earlier three separate house purchases had fallen through forcing him to live at his place of work and his family to stay with relatives. As a result he suffered severe emotional trauma and committed suicide. The insurance company decided that there was no intention to commit suicide when the policies were effected and therefore waived the suicide clause. The full sum assured was paid to the widow and two children. In her own words "Though there is no legal obligation for you to pay any amount to us, your company not only paid the full amount, but the interest also. My children and I feel deeply grateful to your company."

(Source: LIA Booklet 'Living Life to the Full')

Statistics show that many business people operate under extreme stress and worry over finance yet few seem to take steps to insure against it. The market for key man, share protections, loan coverages and pensions is tremendous. They will welcome your ideas and advice.

BUYING INTEREST/CLOSING/INTEREST AROUSERS

I lived in Essex about 17 years ago and one day this chap walked down my drive with a briefcase. He knocked at my door and said "Do you want to see how easy it is for your house to catch fire?" I responded with horror "No I don't".
He said "I can assure you that there will be no risk to you or your family".
I said: "What are you going to do then" at which point he laid his case on the ground and set it alight. He then sprayed this fire extinguisher at the case and put the fire out. Seeing this I said "FANTASTIC, How much is that?" He proceeded to do a twenty minute presentation about fires in the UK without apparently taking a breath. I couldn't take much more of this and said to him "Why didn't you close me on the first buying signal" he looked at me in puzzlement and said "Well what buying signal was that then mate?" I explained to him that when a prospect like me says with enthusiasm "FANTASTIC, How much is that?." It means that they may be interested in buying and he

should home in on the INTEREST.   He said to me "NO, YOU'RE WRONG, AS MY GOVERNOR TELLS ME THAT WHEN A PUNTER SAYS HOW MUCH AT THE START IT MEANS THEY'RE NOT INTERESTED AND YOU KEEP ON UNTIL THEY ARE."

I said that is not true and you must be preoccupied with the price to which he replied:

"Okay you can have two for the price of one." Sometimes we can talk ourselves out of business by simply failing to notice BUYING SIGNALS or making ASSUMPTIONS.

Thankfully I have never had to use those fire extinguishers but it is really nice to know they are there JUST IN CASE.

"I don't know what to do about my financial planning"

5

FACT-FINDING AND PRESENTING CORRECT SOLUTIONS TO NEEDS

We cannot give correct personal advice until we are aware of all the facts. We have to ascertain what the prospect wants, his or her personal requirements and plans for the future.

Setting the Scene

The golden rule in any interview is that you should first clear your mind of any preconceived ideas about the prospect's thoughts and feelings. You should be prepared to listen intelligently and follow any agenda. That doesn't mean, of course, that you shouldn't prepare thoroughly. Find out as much as you can about the prospect's job and other circumstances and use this information as a basis of preparation without being judgemental or assumptive.

Relax the Prospect

Your prospect's name is very important to them and it

is therefore IMPORTANT that you can remember and pronounce it. Repeat it after first hearing and note its pronunciation and spelling. If your call is the result of a referred lead have a card or letter of introduction ready. Before you can recommend a set of proposals to your prospect, common sense and regulations dictates that you must discover all relevant information about their circumstances. A tense and suspicious prospect will not be receptive to questions needed in completing a fact-find. Your first priority must, therefore, be to relax the prospect. Your own social style and that of the prospect will guide you as to the best way to do this. Be friendly, yet professional, confident, not aggressive, respectful yet thorough. But most importantly be you! Be professional and friendly and not over-pushy. Treat the prospects with the respect they deserve.

Finding the Facts

Fill in the financial planning questionnaire. This will be the basis of your recommendations, so it is essential that you compile as much information as you can. Follow the structure but also ask searching questions. For example: "Why did you take out this policy?" "What will happen to the school-fees programme if you die?" "When did you last review the level of your life cover?" "How much will you have to live on after retirement?" "What are your retirement plans?" "Do you plan a big wedding for your daughter?" "Will the children go on to university?" "Are you likely to receive any inheritance, lump sum or compensation in the near future?". Use this opportunity to note potential leads for the future.

A key question must be "Have you made a will?" If the answer is 'yes' you may go on to discuss tax planning and the implications of ignoring this vital area. If a will hasn't been made there is an opportunity to convince them of the wisdom of doing so quickly, and to expand on the problem of dying intestate. Look to write policies under Trust if relevant.

An intelligent and thorough fact-finding session should reveal many opportunities and set the prospect thinking in the right direction. It will also give you a sound basis on which to help the prospect now or in the future. Give them a copy of the fact-find for their personal records or reference and a guide for adequate snapshot planning.

PRESENTING THE CORRECT SOLUTION FOR YOUR PROSPECT'S NEEDS - TEN SUGGESTIONS :

1. **Privacy**
    Whenever possible hold the presentation in private. It is often embarrassing for someone to discuss their own financial situation where others could overhear, such as in cafés and bars.

2. **Paperwork**
    Have all the necessary forms close at hand and keep a pen handy throughout the presentation. This will save time and add to your image of professionalism when it is time to complete the application. Try to use an attractive looking pen, and keep a back-up. Understand the forms and give copies to the client. Use a checklist or agenda to keep you focused.

3. **Position**

   If you can, sit on the same side of the desk or table as the prospect to help complete the forms. It also avoids confrontational body language. Try to use a table or a comfortable chair and make sure it is away from distractions such as the telephone or television. Avoid POWER body language or positioning in a threatening manner

4. **Confidence**

   Be confident. If you've planned your strategy wisely there is no need for nerves. Try to use an agenda and keep to time. Remember your objective. Be professional.

5. **Enthusiasm**

   Be enthusiastic. It's infectious. Believe in your company, your product and your prospect, but don't get carried away with your passion. The client is the important person.

6. **Sell Benefits**

   Always sell benefits which are important to your prospect, not technical features. Your prospect wants to know what the product will do for them. Keep saying "Which means that..." to help them understand these benefits. Check their understanding by asking questions such as "How do you feel about this?" or "Do you think this may be of help to you?" Look for buying intent AT ALL TIMES and question this interest.

7. **Keep it Simple**

   Do not confuse the prospect by presenting too many alternatives. Few of us like complicated rushed decisions. Make it easy on the prospect, but ensure that the facts are clearly   stated, and never exaggerate the benefits to force a sale. Always leave full details for your prospect to read at their leisure.   Honesty is a sound principle and trust essential.

8. **Proposals**

   Present your proposals to the prospect in a logical way, referring back to the fact-find to highlight shortfalls and other areas of concern. Where maximum advantage is not being taken of an Inland Revenue allowance, point it out!

9. **Illustrate: use pictures or anecdotes where possible**

   Be graphic, illustrate your arguments with stories to help the prospect understand the concept you are presenting. Relate to the prospect.

10. **Comply**

    Follow the compliance rules carefully, giving incorrect advice can be costly. The monitoring unit, management supervision and head office checks are there to help you as well as the client. Ask for specialist technical or managerial help whenever you need it.

Much will depend on PRIORITY OF NEED and the Presentation of Solutions will be based on the Fact-Find. The product is merely a means of providing a solution.

What we are here for:

Joe runs his own business and, whilst accepting the need for a pension, has always been sceptical about insurance. One day he rang his financial adviser to say that he needed to raise some extra funds. He achieved this by a simple interest only re-mortgage covered by the existing pension scheme for both life protection and repayment.

Joe was also informed that although he had adequate life cover, he had no protection against loss of health. Because Joe had recently changed from being self-employed to employed status within his own limited company, he could pay his pensions premiums net and the associated tax saving more than covered the premiums on a critical illness policy.

One month later Joe suffered a heart attack, his condition wasn't terminal but he was off work for a long time. As sole proprietor handling his business was difficult, which is where the critical illness policy came in. Everything, down to the payment of the cheque, went like clockwork. Joe's attitude to insurance has now taken a dramatic and positive turn.

(Source: LIA booklet 'Living Life to the Full')

Statistics show that people appreciate critical illness cover only when it's too late. Take out that cover when your health is fine, we never know what is around the corner.

6

CLOSING: COMPLETING THE RECOMMENDATIONS TO THE SATISFACTION OF THE CLIENT

Identifying Closing Opportunities

Closing the sale should be a logical extension of the rest of your presentation. You should always listen out for buying opportunities from the prospect. Questions often point to buying signals.
For example:

"Fantastic, how do I fill in the form?"
"This sounds just what I want."
"Will I need a medical for this?"
"I am really grateful to you for taking the time to do this for me what do I have to do next?"
"What about the tax situation?"
"How soon can we proceed with this?"
"Where do I sign?"
"Will I need to see my accountant over the paperwork or will you do it?"

Your replies to these statements should be positive

and helpful, using the opportunity to return a question to check a point. Avoid wasting the prospects time and close effectively.

"Well, let's see how you look on paper first."
"It has helped many people in similar situations to your own."
"We need to start on the paper work now as it is necessary to gain the tax advantages before the end of the year."

Often you'll have no alternative but to ask the prospect to buy:

"We've looked at your financial situation and found some areas needing urgent attention. We have agreed the solution and the budget to underpin them. All that remains is some paperwork which is essential to enable you to gain the tax advantages or obtain the protection required."

Help your prospect make the right decision. Do not be afraid to ask for the business. **Do not be over pushy.** If the prospect is unhappy, has little money available, or is worried over one aspect, you must understand and treat this respectfully. Give them time to consider but avoid making ASSUMPTIONS. Ask positive open questions, reassure and tell the person the benefits of completing the business.

Overcoming Objections

Identify closing objections and the reason they occur.

I recently read a book on life assurance that was

written over seventy years ago and the most common response was:

"I want to think about it."
The prospect may be uncertain about the recommendation and need reassuring. Ask further questions to check the problem. It may be budget or fear.

We may have made our presentation too complex and worried the prospect about the commitment or pitched the recommendation too high!

When the prospect says he or she wants to think it over there could be any number of reasons for this. Procrastination, from lack of money, to concern about health and exposure to a medical. Your job is to extract the real reason and reassure the person or adjust your recommendation accordingly.

It may be that your presentation was too complex.

You could say: "I think we agreed that you have a financial problem which needs solving urgently and I am happy to discuss plans with your accountant. Is there anything specific concerning you?"

Close the sale positively, help the new client to understand the commitment, benefits and paperwork. Explain the policy once written and thank the client for his business. Remember:
"A sale is not the end, it is the beginning of an ongoing process."

Two other Common Objections

1) "I can't afford it!"

It may be that the cost has worried them.

You could say: "I can understand that you need to balance funding today's needs with those of tomorrow. Let's look again at the most comfortable level for you. Did you realise that the Inland Revenue give you tax relief on your pension contributions to help offset the cost?"

Work through the financial situation for the fact-find to fund solutions.

2) "I need to speak to my accountant."

TEN SUGGESTIONS FOR COPING WITH CLOSING OBJECTIONS

1) Listen before you reply.
2) Use tact, don't get impatient or angry. Remember our Professional Code of Conduct. A call isn't a battle, it may be the start of a professional friendship.
3) Let the prospect voice his or her objections.
4) Do not make assumptions, check it out before you reply.
5) Give positive reinforcement to the objection: "That's a good point." "I can understand your concern." Answer the question, factually and with reinforcement, using visuals if needed, or reassurance resources, such as approved sales aids or press comment.
6) Make sure the prospect is happy with your response.

7) Answer the objection honestly and factually.
8) If the prospect is just NOT INTERESTED it may be better to actually bring the meeting to a close, leaving the possibilities open for a future date.
9) If the prospect is comfortable, you can ask for them to buy. Respect the choice of buying.
   If not, ask if there is anybody else who they think likely to be interested in your service, or make an appointment to see them again later when circumstances have changed.
10) Don't waste your time arguing with the prospect, if you have laid out your recommendations professionally and these meet the outlined needs, you have done a good job and should perhaps charge for time spent!

Why we are here:

Martin had been a photographer for eighteen years. Hardworking, active and continually on the go, he never even considered the likelihood of serious illness. He did, however take out critical illness insurance, thanks to the advice of his financial adviser. This was very fortunate. Martin woke one day to find that he had suffered a stroke in the middle of the night. He spent the next month in hospital, six months on crutches and is now only able to walk with their aid. He is only 38 years old. He is unlikely to ever work again in a full-time capaticy.

Martin received a £60,000 payout from the critical illness policy which paid off his mortgage and removed his biggest single worry - the security of a family home.
(Source: LIA booklet Living Life to the Full')

The
Regulator

The
Product
Provider

The
Adviser

The
Client

All friends working together

7

SERVICING/ADDING VALUE TO EXISTING CLIENTS

"SUCCESS IS SPEAKING WORDS OF PRAISE, IN CHEERING OTHER PEOPLES' WAYS IN DOING THE BEST YOU CAN WITH EVERY TASK AND PLAN"

Sometimes the enthusiastic financial adviser spends a lot of time looking for new clients at the expense of the existing ones. Some very successful advisers work the client bank very well and hardly need to find new clients.

It is essential that we service our clients correctly and keep them informed and reassured - only in this way can we earn our commission or fee. If not, we may lose the client and also have a complaint issued against us. Do not make promises you cannot keep: providing an excellent customer service is one of the most satisfying aspects of our job.

It is important to PRIORITISE our client bank, and regularly review their needs. Our existing client bank is important as not only is it comprised of our satisfied customers, but also as a source of increasing referrals and friendship. Clients circumstances change and we need to help them cope with these changes positively.

• UPDATE 'FACT-FIND' AND 'ADVICE' FREQUENTLY •

Account Management:

The prioritisation of accounts is one way to keep our focus sharp and to ensure that we do give the best possible service to those accounts that need and require it. One idea is to group accounts into three sections, GOLD, SILVER AND BRONZE. The gold accounts get the priority on the basis of a regular newsletter, time spent, calls, corporate entertainment and practice attention. The clients may be demanding due to the complexity of the advice given or be the best friends we have and key advocates of our services.

An Italian called Pareto had the theory that 80% of business came from 20% of one's connections, not in those actual words but effectively so. This 80/20 rule strangely seems often to be the case and we must keep our good friends satisfied or they will move on. By giving the GOLD accounts above average service, we ensure that we keep out confidence and professional pride intact.

The SILVER accounts are less demanding but still receive above average service as they could become future advocates of our practice. Indeed, the majority of our clients will be in the silver category. They have fairly basic needs with simple adequate provision, they do not need updates as often as the gold accounts.

The last category is the BRONZE section, the occasional clients who may have completed the odd piece of business, have low priorities or demands.

They may have moved abroad or become incapacitated due to illness, redundancy or other circumstances. They are obviously still valuable to us as clients and require occasional calls. At times we may need to review the bronze accounts and perhaps pass them onto a local colleague or telesales support. However, I firmly believe that if a client becomes incapacitated or suffers hard times, we must show genuine sympathy, compassion and try to help as best we can. This is a fundamental principle of the standards we advocate in our industry.

Database:

There are many excellent computer software database packages available today, especially as which can help categorise clients into areas of occupation, geography, type and also give us essential information to help us give good service. In the USA they are excellent at database management and if you visit that country, call into one of the many software business shops and browse around. The development of computer software has been remarkable in recent years and the computer is a valuable tool which helps us to keep in contact with our clients, access information or make calculations. With the complexity of certain aspects of the financial services markets it is necessary to be able to access technical information, be updated or be able to prepare accurate reports. Some people say they are not computer literate and cannot work the things. That being the case, employ the help of somebody who can! Alternatively, you could go on a training course, or better still simply 'have a go'. I found that once I was 'hands on' the computer became much less of a problem and more of a friend.

However, try to avoid becoming addicted to the computer, internet or the continual advancements as it is merely a resource to help us do our job of client contact and financial advising. A century ago even the telephone was not regularly used in our profession.

The Future:

There is no doubt that telecommunications, computers and electronics will become even more fascinating as we move into the 21st century and our pioneers from those coffee houses in the 18th century, could perhaps never have dreamed of the wonders seen today, which we so often take for granted.

Scientific advancements in the areas of medicine, electronics and almost every sector of our lives has meant that the insurance industry has faced considerable challenges, moved with the times and tried very hard to give the correct customer care. Perhaps we will soon see client reviews by telecommunication, internet or whatever. But remember, personal contact is an essential element and will still be needed to help our friends cope with the emotional demands of being human beings and not machines.

History shows that we often experience cyclical events and return to the old ways of simplicity, even if for novelty value. I was reading a book recently which was first publishd in 1929 and the basics were just the same as today, except we now tend to live longer or differently.

Peace of Mind:

Financial planning is about peace of mind. Statistics show that many people do not manage their investments or allowances, use the wrong investment agents and get low interest. They need help to fill in their financial questionnaires and encouragement to undertake regular reviews.

Charles Kingsley said:
"If I have made one human being at least a little wiser, happier or better this day, I know I have done my duty."
How true this is in client servicing!

Why we are here:

A client decided to start a directors pension plan placing a considerable amount of money with a leading life office. Every year the adviser called and reassured the director and updated the plan to meet his requirements. The director eventually decided to sell the business and retired very satisfied with the return on the pension plan. Thanking the adviser for the time he had spent on the review and the help he had given. This is a typical story about the many satisfied clients, who were well looked after by their advisers. They had received the respect and time deserved for the large investment made. The adviser had also been fair on the charges and commissions to ensure that his client had good value. He had arranged a good balance between monthly premium and large single premiums and been open with the client well before the regulations insisted.

8

LITTLE STORIES AND TIPS

Household Budgets

We may have a freezer and a washing machine in our kitchen. Presumably they are insured under our household contents policy. Imagine we had another machine in our kitchen and every week we could push a button and out came fifty pound notes. In case something went wrong we would want to insure it, to make sure that we could go on getting our income, wouldn't we? Well we do have such a machine sitting right here. How much should we cover ourselves for?

How much do we spend on car insurance each year? If it was damaged in a car crash that insurance would allow the car to be replaced, if we had died in that crash our family may not have sufficient income to run the car! Which is more imporant - insuring your car or insuring your income Obviously BOTH.

A premium is the collateral on a loan your family will not need.

If we had a goose which laid golden eggs, which would we insure, the eggs or the goose?

Insurance provides peace of mind for little outlay and should be an essential family and business budget item.

The pyramid of life

To illustrate the financial disaster facing many families draw the pyramid of life for your prospect. Point out that it is only income which is keeping the family at its current standard of living. Take away the income and the family begins to slide down to lower standards of living. "How far down will you allow your family to fall?"

IT IS YOUR REMIT TO ADVISE MEMBERS OF THE PUBLIC OF THEIR NEED FOR BASIC INSURANCE AGAINST POVERTY IN RETIREMENT AN UNTIMELY DEATH OR ILL HEALTH.

Critical Illness/Income Replacement

"Most people are not excited about their own death or serious illness."
"If you had a serious illness how would your family/business cope?"
"How would you cope if your partner contracted a serious illness?"
"I know you worry about catching a disease, so insure against it, just in case..."
"Many serious illnesses can now be cured but are financially disastrous if one is running a business."
"Life assurance does cost money but pays out considerably more when it is most needed, cost is relative."

Pensions

The difference between a happy and an unhappy retirement is often financial. We all get old and need to fund for the future, start as early as possible, save as much as you can, and reap the rewards later on in life. Time goes by and we need income to survive. The Help the Aged and Age Concern charities adverts endorse the need for adequate pension, a concern for the plight of the elderly.

Reluctant to save

Emphasise the benefits of pension planning. Calculate the number of paydays until retirement - 20 years seems a long time, 240 payslips brings it down to size.

Put it to your prospect - "Would you go on a long ocean voyage without lifeboats? Retirement is like a long voyage, you don't know how long it will last. Without this pension plan you will be going on a voyage without lifeboats." Cut out advertisments showing the need. Read the LIA's excellent Industry Realities True Case Study Book on Pensions. Remember the benefits of having a decent income at retirement. Show the minimum and maximum figures and ask the prospect at which point to start, taking into account his full financial need, and satisfaction. State the advantages of increases and augmentation by lump sums at regular times to quickly build up the fund.

Most working people should consider saving into a pension plan. Read the sales literature for specific ideas and use the approved sales aids specially made to help you and the client.   Avoid pensions 'mis-selling' pitfalls.

Investment

Look for a sound balance. Compare the loss due to taxation on Bank deposits, Building Society accounts, and shares with the more tax efficient products.   To illustrate good balanced investments draw a graph and ask the prospect to select the point where they feel comfortable, the right balance between reward and security.   The Government give generous allowances on certain products, point these out to the prospect and explain why they are there.

Cost of Delay

To illustrate the cost of delay in starting a pension, take two quotes to the presentation, one for the prospect's actual age, the other for a person a year older.   Emphasise that it is never too late to start saving for the future, suggest part of their disposable income is saved now.

Always sell the benefits of reasonable contributions and favourable tax treatment. However, take care not to over-commit the client.   Use a lump sum to augment the pension plan and gain tax advantages. Show the MAXIMUM contribution possible quoting the Inland Revenue limits, but let the prospect decide on a level they are comfortable with.

We should remember that the important aspects are:

- the level of contribution relative to income
- the immediate and future tax benefits

- an awareness of the future problems assoicated with low income
- utilization of other income and investment opportunities to take advantage of the generous tax concessions.
- technical considerations
- best advice

Young Prospects

When speaking to younger prospects remember that a pension can conjure up visions of old age!

"The only money we may have when we retire is the money we have sent on ahead - do not rely on winning the lottery!" *Tempus fugits.*

Prepare a plan to give flexability to the young prospect and fair charges. With the increasing number of redundancies many people are opting for early retirement and need to start planning early. There are also people who never stop working but need a contingency plan just in case'.

When you have reached agreement on a level of contribution to a pension explain that the contribution will enjoy tax relief and other benefits plus life assurance protection and prospects of early retirement.

Directors Pensions

"Mr(s) Managing Director, if you want to take money out of your company you face the following taxes..." show the prospect a list." If I could show you a way in which you could set up a subsidiary company for your benefit alone without any of these taxes I know you would be interested"

This tax exempt subsidiary company is in fact a director's company pension scheme. The advantages of a directors pension scheme are ones that every successful director should consider. Tax is not the only positive reason why, especially under small self-administered schemes or the flexible arrangements on offer nowadays to help them. Use single preiums to give future encashment potential, at low charges, if needed. Directors need a contingency fund for the future.

Employee Pension Schemes

A simple pension can be achieved by setting up a group scheme with the employer paying a contribution, tax deductible, and the employee augmenting this. Individual member fact-finds and interviews help sell the benefit, and the employers endorsement is very welcome.

There are many small companies keen to look after their staff, waiting for somebody to advise them of the options. It could be you! Do not switch existing arrangements without taking care on the detail, or having sufficient technical knowledge of the switch options, as it can be complex and disadvantageous to the client.

Many Successful Businesses are Run by Ordinary Down to Earth People

An accountant friend of mine asked me if I would mind travelling to see a very wealthy famous company which manufactured some well known sports equipment. It was a family business and they were keen to start a pension plan. I arrived after the long journey feeling rather tired and was shocked to see this family, bearing a close resemblance to the family in Emmerdale Farm who are always in trouble. I couldn't believe that this ill behaved cursing family of big lads and a dad who looked like a 'mobster' were the owners. They 'took the mickey' out of me and said they were not interested in a pension as their business could be sold at retirement for a great deal of money. I left feeling that the 186 mile round trip was a waste of time, but when I returned, the accountant said they had liked me and they wondered why I hadn't CLOSED the deal. I had assumed they were not interested and left feeling fed up with their insults, instead of understanding their sense of humour and style. Looks are not everything and we should NEVER SIMPLY 'JUDGE A BOOK BY ITS' COVER'

Could Your Family Cope with the Loss of Income?

Suppose that you didn't get paid this week or next, or for several months? How would you get along? Could your family manage any better if your salary never came in again?

"If you're having a tough time getting by on your salary, how well do you think your family will get by without it?"

"If you wouldn't want to live the rest of your life on the face amount of your present insurance, why do you expect your family to?"

"Many young people now attend university and parents can ill afford to support them. Start saving now..."

"All family people need protection, insurance and a plan for the future. Sadly divorce or death can upset these plans and help is needed to reassess the situation when the contingency occurs."

Accidents Will Happen

People die every day and nearly always prematurely. Accidents DO happen, sadly when we least expect them. Be prepared!

Winston Churchill said words to the effect that "If I had my way I would write 'Insurance' above the door of every cottage in England, because for sacrifices which are small, families can be protected against catastrophe which might otherwise wipe them out forever."

Be proud to be in the insurance business. It is there to help us cope with unexpected contingencies.

The time we appreciate the real value of insurance is when we have to face a claim and we never know when that insured catastrophe may hit us.

I had never claimed on my household insurance policy in over thirty years as, thankfully, I had not experienced the horrors of fire or damage so well protrayed in those famous television adverts. On returning home recently from a roadshow I was shocked to see that my house had been struck by lightning on the TV aerial. The inside of the roof was blackened and the TV, video, stereo and my beloved karaoke machine were "wiped out!" I thought THANK GOD THE DAMAGE WAS NOT MORE SEVERE AND THAT I AM INSURED. Thank God I didn't act on those letters and adverts sent to me about cutting the cost of my cover. I stayed with my insurer on full new replacement value and was grateful for the way the claim was settled. I learned that YOU GET THE COVER YOU PAY FOR and IT IS THE WAY THE CLAIM IS SETTLED WHICH IS IMPORTANT, NOT THE SAVING OF A FEW POUNDS IN PREMIUMS. Had I switched to a cheaper policy it may have given me OLD FOR OLD and how much do you think my ten year old equipment would have been worth? We have to watch the small print and policy conditions to judge the real value when we experience a claim.

Plan Now for Tomorrow

Ask any Pensioner whether they have enough income and wished they had saved more.

Help prospects plan for the future and have a financial snapshot of the present

More good things are lost by indecision than by wrong decision

Don't speak of life insurance as a luxury. Are food, clothing and shelter luxuries? They're what life insurance provides.

Ask any widow about the need for life assurance.

One person in five is too ill to work for three months or more.

Accidents happen to seven million people each year.

A single person's State incapacity benefit amounts to very little: could you live on it?

Only one in ten families are covered by some form of health insurance.

It Costs Less Than You Think

People often spend more at the pub or on cigarettes than they do on insurance.

Life insurance costs less to buy than not to buy.

When Life insurance is actually needed, it sometimes can't be purchased at any price.

Enjoy a Healthy and Wealthy Retirement

What do you want to retire on, your bad investment experience or your investment income?

When you retire, it won't be important to know how much money you earned, just how much you saved.

Will you last as long as your mortgage?

Do you want to enjoy holidays when you retire or would you rather sit at home all day?

The basic state pension is very low, could you live on it?

By 2030 it is forecast that there will be just two workers supporting one retired person.

70% of retired people wished they had started a pension sooner.

25% of working people have no pension.

49% of those who do contribute less than £50 per month.

Spouses Need Life Cover Too

Some might not believe in life insurance but beneficiaries always do.

Divorce is common nowadays and there is an increase in single parent families.

Women often earn more than men and are under insured as they sometimes rely on their husbands. Husband and wife are equal, treat them that way.

You Have Valuable Advice To Give

We are trained and have valuable resources to help the clients. Accountants and solicitors do a good job but may not be experienced in insurance or financial planning. Sell your services to them and help them set up a plan for themselves as they are often high earners with specific needs.

Remember life offices have much technical expertise, often free to the client.

Look for topical press articles, cut them out, compile them and use them to learn from, or to help, clients.

Be more INTERESTED than INTERESTING, although

a balance is needed.

Send clients 'good wishes' notices and keep them informed of good news, find common ground.

Use an agenda at meetings and ensure you remind clients of the need.

Keep a success log and a file of 'thank you' letters as indeed other businesses do with their success stories.

If you want time to think something out, MAKE AN APPOINTMENT WITH YOURSELF to create that invaluable time. If you wish, take time to meditate, pray and reflect.

UNDER PROMISE and OVER DELIVER.

Look for good news and be proud of our great industry.

Human Behaviour

We are by nature intelleigent complete animals with wonderful imaginations, capabilities and behaviour patterns. Some of us have variable styles due to our upbringing or habits and it is important for us to be able to recognise these differences in our clients. Some like facts and figures while others prefer brief direct responses. Others just like to chat and some listen. Business people tend to be busy and generally people adapt to their chosen professions.

We are wonderful adaptions and creatures of habit, but equally are often controlled by strong emotion which can throw logic to the wind. Yes, clients can become JEALOUS, GREEDY, ANGRY or SENTIMENTAL. We need to understand this and react accordingly. That is one of the joys of being in a PEOPLE business. We need to acquire sound people skills to be a success.

Contract Flexibility

Modern contracts are fundamentally much more flexible nowadays thanks to technology, but with flexibility also comes confusion or problems. Remember why the product was sold and for what reason, but also explain some of the key flexible items specific to the client. E.g. if they have young children, the childrens options will be more relevant to them than for elderly clients.

Sometimes our industry concentrates too much on price competitiveness and not enough on the flexibility or costs needed to give that service. Ruskin said in the last century words to the effect that "We get what we pay for."

I like flexibility, options and better levels of cover but equally I also like the good old basic products I purchased 30 years ago, long term products as well as short term flexibility.

The value of some of these old plans has proved remarkable, even if inflation has eroded part of the expectation. There are many happy customers well pleased with the return on long term plans for the low premiums paid, also as a result of inflation. So update these customers and reassure them of the current long term values, move away from selling purely on COST to VALUE.

What we are here for:

A Company wanted to help one of their employees, a young contracts manager.

So a small personal pension plan and a health insurance contract were set up on his behalf. The young manager was very fit, played regular rugby and was a non smoker. He also worked very hard for the Company.

Sadly less than a year later he had a dizzy spell and was diagnosed as having had a mild stroke which partially paralysed one side of his body. He was advised to give up driving but since his health policy covered the risk he was able to claim and he was also covered under the pension premium waiver benefit as he could no longer carry out his occupation.

Soon afterwards his employer unfortunately went out of business for unrelated reasons but of course the essential insurance cover was unaffected by this and this help show the Power of Insurance.

He is pleased to recommend similar cover to his friends.

As Winston Churchill said in his famous quotation about the benefits of insurance, mentioned earlier in this book:

"Insurance helps protect people against catastrophes, which may otherwise smash them up for ever and it is our duty to help address this ghastly waste".

Ralph Waldo Emerson also said of SUCCESS.

"To endure false critics and look for the best in others
To know that one life has breathed easier because you
have lived".

In this uncertain world we never know when
catastrophes will hit us and it makes sense to pay a
few pounds in insurance JUST IN CASE.

It also makes sense to SAVE FOR THE FUTURE OR
UNFORESEEN CONTINGENCIES.

To invest savings in a cost effective manner and to
look for sensible advice.

AND FINALLY...
Action Plans/Business Plans

It is important that we have a plan to follow to ensure
our business is successful. We need to work every
day at our Priorities, Goals and Mission Statement.
We need to use our time effectively and this could
include delegating or asking for help when needed.

There are some excellent books on Goal Setting, Time
Management and Business Planning, but much of the
action will be based on your personal desire to
complete your goals as well as the pride you have in
the quality of your advice.

Remember, you must have BELIEF in yourself, in
your services, in your clients AND in the markets.

You must work to a PLAN
You must use all the RESOURCES available.
You must get a balance in your life to enjoy your success, as well as bringing happiness to yourself, your family and your clients.
You need to achieve your own personal GOALS.

Good luck with all of your challenges and please write to me with new positive stories, via my Publisher or LIA headquarters.

Paul Joslyn

SOME INDUSTRY REALITIES

- Over two thirds of all households - around 17 million homes - are protected by life insurance.

- At the start of 1994 there were 39 million ordinary life policies and 46 million industrial life policies in force in the UK, total sums assured of over £700 billion - £15,000 for every adult in the country.

- In 1993, £30 billion was paid out to life insurance policyholders and a further £13 billion in pensions scheme periodical payment, claims following a death, lump sums or refunds.

- Around 7 million employees are in occupational schemes covered by life insurance companies.

- Over 18 million individual personal pension policies are in force.

- Life insurance and pension funds account for half the total financial assets of the personal sector. That's more than three times the deposits held in banks and building societies.

A few recent critical illness claims

Sex	Age at	Occupation Claim	Reason for Claim	Amount paid
F	35	Legal Administrator	Cancer	£57,082
F	53	Shop Assistant	Rheumatoid Arthritis	£50,000
M	45	Financial Adviser	Heart Attack	£50,000
M	38	Teacher	Brain Tumour	£75,000
M	29	Lighting Manager	Hodgkin's Disease	£100,000
M	41	Community Worker	Stroke	£78,500.

Source LIA "Industry Realities" booklet

BE PROUD OF OUR GREAT PROFESSION

ALWAYS SELL TO NEEDS AND LOOK AFTER THE BEST INTERESTS OF YOUR CUSTOMERS.

BE ENTHUSIASTIC, HAVE EMPATHY AND BE EFFECTIVE.

ENJOY YOUR PROFESSIONAL SUCCESS AND TELL ALL YOUR FAMILY AND FRIENDS. WE LIKE WINNERS.